He's Never Heard of You, Either

Doonesbury books by G. B. Trudeau

Still a Few Bugs in the System
The President Is a Lot Smarter Than You Think
But This War Had Such Promise
Call Me When You Find America
Guilty, Guilty, Guilty!
"What Do We Have for the Witnesses, Johnnie?"
Dare To Be Great, Ms. Caucus
Wouldn't a Gremlin Have Been More Sensible?
"Speaking of Inalienable Rights, Amy . . ."
You're Never Too Old for Nuts and Berries
An Especially Tricky People
As the Kid Goes for Broke
Stalking the Perfect Tan
"Any Grooming Hints for Your Fans, Rollie?"
But the Pension Fund Was Just Sitting There
We're Not Out of the Woods Yet
A Tad Overweight, but Violet Eyes to Die For
And That's My Final Offer!
He's Never Heard of You, Either

In Large Format

The Doonesbury Chronicles
Doonesbury's Greatest Hits

a Doonesbury book by

G B Trudeau

He's Never Heard of You, Either

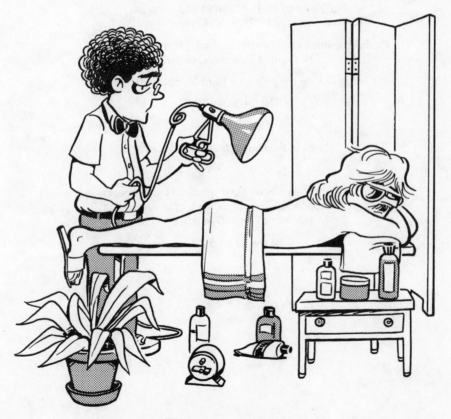

An Owl Book 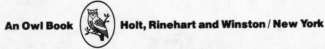 Holt, Rinehart and Winston / New York

Published by Holt, Rinehart and Winston, 383 Madison Avenue, New York, New York 10017.

Published simultaneously in Canada by Holt, Rinehart and Winston of Canada, Limited.

Library of Congress Catalog Card Number: 80-84426

ISBN: 0-03-049196-7

First Edition

Printed in the United States of America

The cartoons in this book have appeared in newspapers in the United States and abroad under the auspices of Universal Press Syndicate.

2 4 6 8 10 9 7 5 3 1

GOOD EVENING. TODAY THE CANDIDATES FOR PRESIDENT HELD A JOINT NEWS CONFERENCE TO MAKE AN URGENT APPEAL FOR NATIONAL DISCORD. JUDY WOODRUFF HAS DETAILS.

THEY CALL IT "DISUNITY DAY." LED BY GOVERNOR JOHN CONNALLY, THE MAJOR CANDIDATES OFFICIALLY CALLED OFF THEIR SELF-IMPOSED BAN ON CRITICIZING PRESIDENT CARTER'S FOREIGN POLICY.

CHARGING THAT CARTER HAD UNFAIRLY TAKEN ADVANTAGE OF THE BAN BY RALLYING THE COUNTRY BEHIND HIM, CONNALLY SAID HE WAS "SICK AND TIRED OF PUTTING HOSTAGES AHEAD OF POLITICS."

THE CALL FOR DISUNITY IS EXPECTED TO RECEIVE BIPARTISAN SUPPORT.

GBTrudeau

GBTrudeau

OVER THE YEARS, WE'VE HAD HIGH PROFILES AND WE'VE HAD LOW PROFILES, BUT FEW SILHOUETTES HAVE LINGERED SO LONG ON THE CULTURAL LANDSCAPE AS THAT OF SEXUAL EXPLORATEUR GAY TALESE.

MR. TALESE IS JUST BACK FROM A NINE-YEAR SAFARI THROUGH THE PORN SHOPS AND MASSAGE PARLORS OF AMERICA, AND HE HAS PUT HIS FINDINGS IN HIS NEW BOOK, "THY NEIGHBOR'S WIFE." MR. TALESE, WHAT'S THE BOOK ABOUT?

WELL, BY WAY OF ANSWERING, IF I MAY, I'D LIKE TO READ SELECTED PASSAGES FROM THE BOOK ITSELF.

WE WERE HOPING YOU'D SAY THAT, MR. TALESE. TAKE IT AWAY.

"IN THE BEGINNING, GAY TALESE DIDN'T EVEN OWN A RAINCOAT.."

YOU'RE KIDDING!

"AS TALESE EMERGED FROM HIS '57 TRIUMPH, HIS EYES LOOKED UP HUNGRILY AT THE FLICKERING RED NEON SIGN THAT READ 'LIVE NUDE CO-EDS'.."

"HE BOUNDED UP THE THREE FLIGHTS OF STEPS, ANXIOUS TO KEEP HIS APPOINTMENT WITH THE VOLUPTUOUS CHEMISTRY MAJOR WHOSE PHOTO HE HAD SELECTED WITH SUCH CARE FROM THE MASSAGE PARLOR PICTURE BOOK."

"WHEN THEY WERE FINALLY ALONE TALESE TURNED TO HER AND SAID, 'I WANT TO JOIN YOUR SILENT REVOLUTION OF THE SENSES, YOUR DEPARTURE FROM CONVENTIONALITY.' THE MASSEUSE SMILED AND REACHED FOR THE POWDER."

"MEANWHILE, OUT IN THE CAR, TALESE'S WIFE WAS GROWING IMPATIENT.."

UNDERSTANDABLY!